Easy
Christian Crafts
Grades 1-3

By
Linda Standke

Cover illustration by
Jack Snider

Inside illustrations by
Julie Anderson

Carson-Dellosa Christian Publishing

Scripture taken from the HOLY BIBLE: NEW INTERNATIONAL VERSION®. NIV®. Copyright © 1973, 1978, 1984 by International Bible Society. Used by permission of Zondervan Publishing House.

The "NIV" and "New International Version" trademarks are registered in the United States Patent and Trademark Office by International Bible Society.

Credits:
Author: Linda Standke
Project Director: Sherrill B. Flora
Editors: Sherrill B. Flora, D'Arlyn Marks, Sharon Thompson
Cover Illustration: Jack Snider
Cover Design: Annette Hollister-Papp
Inside Illustrations: Julie Anderson

Printed in the USA · All Rights Reserved   ISBN 0-88724-795-4

Introduction

This book was designed for parents, home educators, and Sunday school and Christian school educators who want to provide fun and rewarding craft projects that teach young children about God's love.

The Bible will come alive for children in meaningful ways as they create a two-foot ark, learn about Daniel's faith by making prayer cards and a prayer card holder, and build a shoe box stable for the birth of Jesus. The projects included in this book not only allow children to learn Bible truth from easy-to-make craft projects, but they also provide children with play experiences that promote the telling and retelling of favorite Bible stories.

Each craft project begins with a scripture reference and a short summary to help guide the parent/teacher. Read the entire Biblical passage, discuss its meaning with the children and then follow up with the craft activity.

It is the author's hope that as you guide the children through these craft projects, they will learn about and experience God's love.

Contents

Creation on a Stick

Genesis 1

Read the children the story of creation from a children's Bible. Our God designed a beautiful world for us. It took God six days to form our earth and on the seventh day God rested. Celebrate each day of creation by making this project. The children will be able to retell the story of creation using these stick patterns.

Materials Needed:

* 7 tongue depressors per student
* 1 plastic ready-made frosting container (empty & washed) per student
* Scissors
* Crayons or markers
* Tape
* 2 sheets white construction paper or card stock per student

Directions:

1. Wash and completely dry the empty frosting containers.
2. Copy the days of creation patterns found on pages 5 & 6 onto white construction paper or card stock. Each student should have the seven days of creation patterns and the container pattern.
3. Give each of the children seven tongue depressors. Have the children print the numerals 1 through 7 on each of their tongue depressors.
4. Have the children color the days of creation patterns and cut them out.
5. The children should match each creation picture to the appropriate numbered stick. Tape the pattern to the back of the stick. Make sure the number of the pattern and the number on the tongue depressor are on the same side.
6. Have each child color the container pattern, cut it out, wrap it around the frosting container, and secure it with tape.
7. Place the creation sticks in the container.

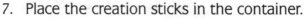

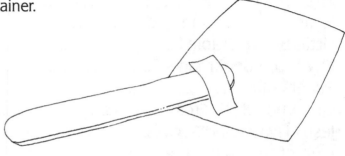

5. Make sure the number of the pattern and the number on the tongue depressor are on the same side.

Creation on a Stick Patterns

Day 1

Day

He separated the light from dark...

Night

Day 2

He called the expanse "sky."

Day 3

"Let the land produce vegetation..."

"He called water "sea"...

"He called the dry ground "land"...

Day 4

a greater light, the sun

a lesser light, the moon

and the stars

Creation on a Stick Patterns

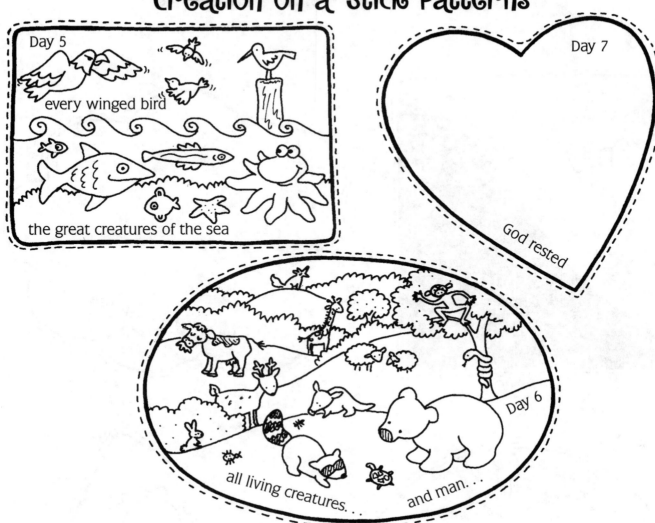

Day 5

every winged bird

the great creatures of the sea

Day 7

God rested

all living creatures...

and man...

Day 6

Container cover: extend paper to 10.5.˝ Total measurement of container wrap should be 3.25˝ x 10.5.˝

Giant Noah's Ark

Genesis 6

Noah and the Ark is a favorite Bible story of young children. Creating this giant ark, the animals, and Noah's family will provide the children with a great art experience, and the children will have a lot of fun retelling this wonderful Bible story.

Materials Needed:

* 1 sheet of 17˝x 24˝ tagboard (ark) for each child
* 7 sheets of card stock for each child
* Markers or crayons
* Scissors
* Tape
* *Optional:* brown paint & paintbrush for ark

Directions:

1. Using the ark example given (see illustration on page 8), mark and cut the tagboard to create an ark. The ark will stand when you fold along the dotted lines. Cut the door to create a ramp for the animals to enter the ark.
2. Paint or color the ark.
3. Copy, color, and cut out the animal and people patterns found on pages 8-14.
4. Fold along the dotted lines to make your characters stand.
5. Retell the story of Noah and have the animals actually enter the ark through the open door.

Giant Noah's Ark Patterns

Tagboard Guide
Enlarge and use this pattern as your guide. Mark the tagboard as shown and cut on solid lines.
Stand the ark by folding on the dotted lines and by creating a ramped door.

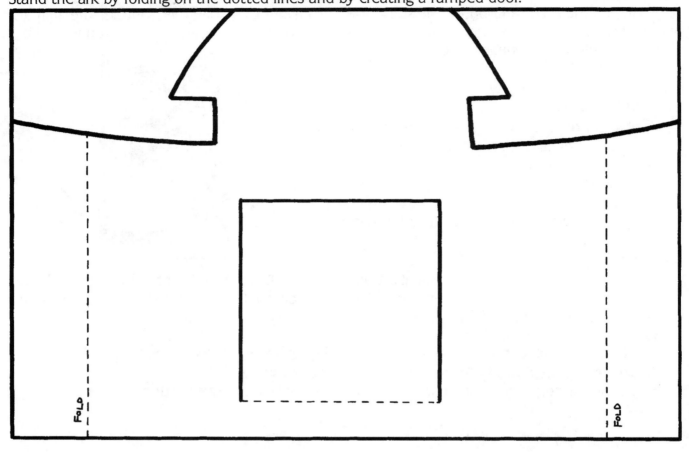

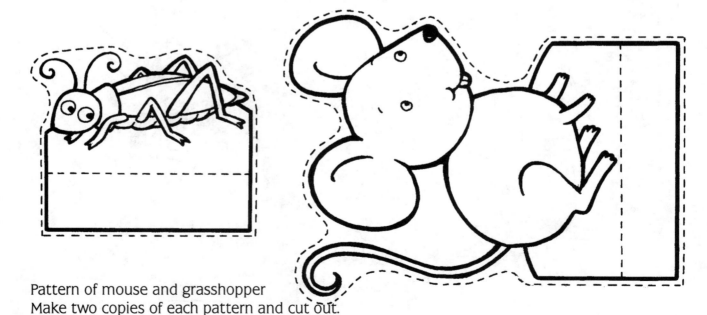

Pattern of mouse and grasshopper
Make two copies of each pattern and cut out.

Giant Noah's Ark Patterns

Copy and cut out Noah and his wife.

Giant Noah's Ark Patterns

Make three copies of this pattern and cut out. Color each couple a different color to represent Noah's three sons (Shem, Ham, and Japheth) and daughters-in-law.

Giant Noah's Ark Patterns

Copy two elephants and cut out.

Giant Noah's Ark Patterns

Copy two giraffes and cut out. Glue or tape the head onto the body to create a "tall" giraffe.

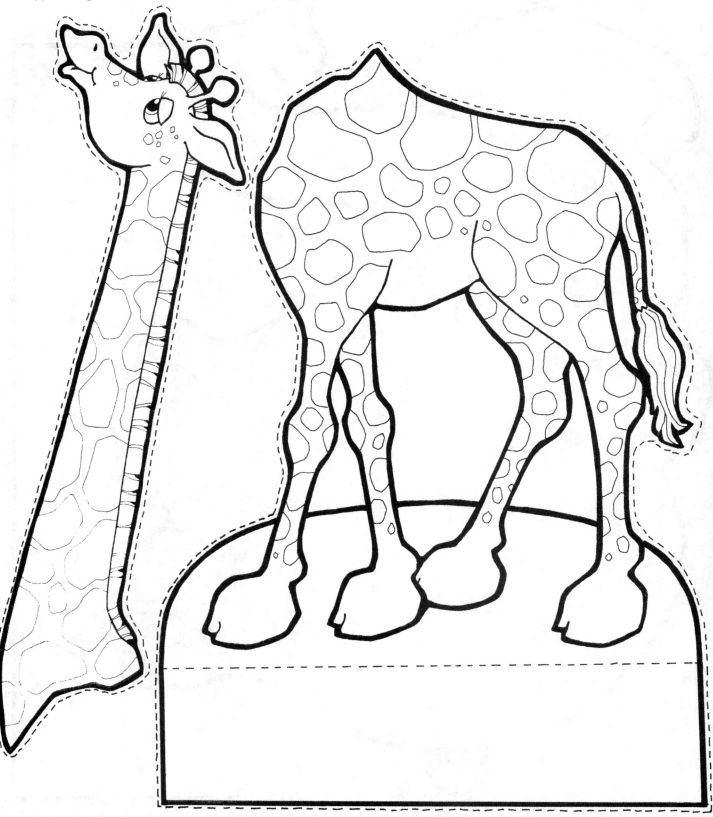

Giant Noah's Ark Patterns

Copy and cut out the birds.

Copy and cut out the lion and lioness.

Easy Christian Crafts Gr. 1-3

Giant Noah's Ark Patterns

Copy two alligators and two bears and cut out.

Mosaic Rainbow

Genesis 9

The beautiful rainbow is our reminder of God's covenant to us that the earth will never be flooded again. Children will love creating their own colorful mosaic rainbows by simply tearing construction paper and gluing it onto their pattern.

Materials Needed:

* Pink, red, orange, yellow, green, blue and purple construction paper
* Gluesticks
* Paper punch
* Yarn
* Card stock
* Scissors

Directions:

1. Copy the rainbow pattern found on page 16 onto card stock for each child. Cut out the rainbow pattern along the dotted lines.
2. Have children tear construction paper into little pieces. Remind them that they will be gluing the colored pieces onto their rainbow. Keep the paper in piles according to color.
3. Using gluesticks, glue each piece of paper to the rainbow according to color.
4. When the rainbow is totally filled with colored paper, use the paper punch to make a hole in the top center of the rainbow for hanging.
5. Cut yarn into length desired, thread through hole, and tie to create a loop for hanging.
6. Hang each child's rainbow and remind them that this is God's promise to each of us.

2. Keep the paper in piles according to color.

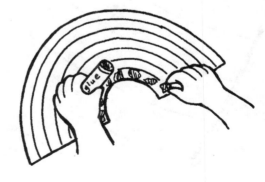

3. Glue each piece of paper to the rainbow according to color.

Mosaic Rainbow Pattern

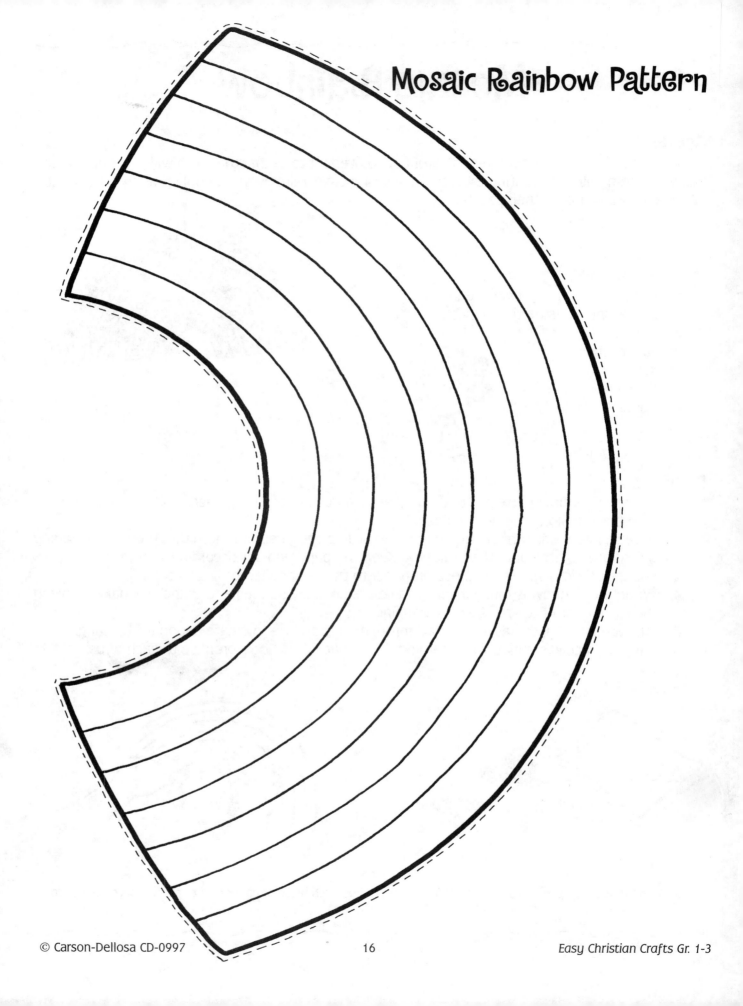

Joseph's Coat of Many Colors

Genesis 37

God has a special plan for each one of us. Joseph trusted God to guide him even though he did not know what God's plan was for him. Cutting and matching these colored shapes will create a coat of many colors. The coat should remind us of the truth that God is watching over each of us, no matter where we are or what is happening in our lives.

Materials Needed:

* ✳ White construction paper or card stock
* ✳ Crayons
* ✳ Scissors
* ✳ Gluesticks
* ✳ *Optional:* you can use colored glitter to fill in the spaces on the coat instead of paper

Directions:

1. Copy the pattern found on page 18 onto white construction paper. One coat pattern for each child. (*Optional:* if you have a limited amount of time, the children can simply color Joseph's coat on page 18.)
2. Copy the coat shape patterns found on page 19 onto various colors of construction paper. (The goal is to have a wide assortment of colored shapes.)
3. Cut out the shapes and glue them to the matching shape on the coat.

Joseph's Coat of Many Colors

Joseph's Coat of Many Colors Shape Patterns

Friendship Frame

1 Samuel 20

David and Jonathan were best friends. They both loved God very much. Sharing your faith with a friend is very special. Make these friendship frames and celebrate your friendships. Do not forget to put a picture of a friend in it, or give it as a gift with a framed picture of yourself.

Materials Needed:
* White and colored construction paper
* Scissors
* Gluesticks
* Markers
* Photograph

Directions:

The frame is intended for a traditional 4˝ x 6˝ photograph. Adjust the size of the photo display if using a 3˝ x 5˝ or Polaroid photograph.

1. Copy and cut the main frame pattern found on page 21 from any color construction paper.
2. Copy the frame decorative border strip patterns and stabilizing strip found on page 22 onto white paper.
3. Cut and glue the decorations to the frame as shown.
4. Place the photograph on the back of frame and tape.
5. Mount the stabilizer strip by folding on the dotted lines and taping to the two insides of the frame. Make sure you evenly match the bottom of the frame with the stabilizer strip.

1. Copy and cut out frame.

3. Decorate and glue the borders to the frame.

4. Place the photograph on the back of the frame and tape.

5. Tape the stabilizer strip in place.

Friendship Frame Pattern

Main Frame   Copy, cut along the solid lines and fold on dotted line.

fold

cut out

Friendship Frame Patterns

Patterns of the decorative side borders. Copy, cut out, color, and glue on the frame.

Stabilizer
Copy and cut out.

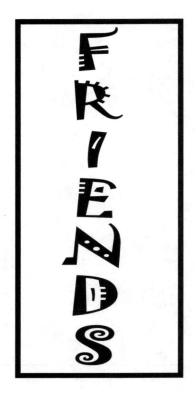

top border

bottom border

Copy, cut out, color, and glue on the frame.

Prayer Power Cards

Daniel 2

Daniel refused to stop praying to God even though the king made a decree that he stop. Daniel knew there was only one true God. These simple prayer cards will help children remember Daniel's story and how important it is to keep God first in their lives.

Materials Needed:
* 1 paper lunch bag per child
* Gold, brown, or yellow yarn
* Card stock
* Glue
* Scissors
* Markers

Directions:
1. With paper bag folded shut, measure 4.5˝ from the bottom and cut off the top of the bag. (See illustration.)
2. Copy and cut out the bag patterns found on page 24 and the prayer cards found on pages 24 through 27.
3. Color the lion head and glue it to one side of the still-folded bag. This will be the front.
4. Cut gold or yellow yarn into 1.5˝ pieces for the lion's mane.
5. With the bag still folded flat (for easy working), attach lion's mane by gluing the yarn around the lion's head. Encourage children to have their yarn pieces touching each other on the mane so that it looks full. Continue around the head until completed. Let the glue dry.
6. Cut out the prayer cards on solid lines. Children may choose to color the border.
7. Open the bag and place prayer cards inside.

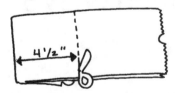

1. Cut off the top of the bag.

3. Color the lion head and glue it to one side of the still-folded bag.

5. Glue yarn around the lion's head.

6. Cut out the prayer cards on solid lines.

Lion's head.
Glue to front of bag

Card 1

Glue to back of bag.

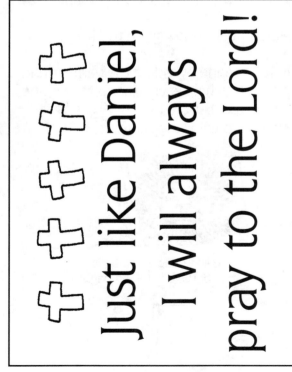

Just like Daniel,
I will always
pray to the Lord!

I will pray to the Lord!

Dear Lord,
I am so
thankful
that you
will always
love me.
Amen

Prayer Power Cards Patterns

Card 2

I will pray to the Lord!

Dear God,
Please help
me remember
that loving you
is more
important
than anything
else.
Amen

Card 3

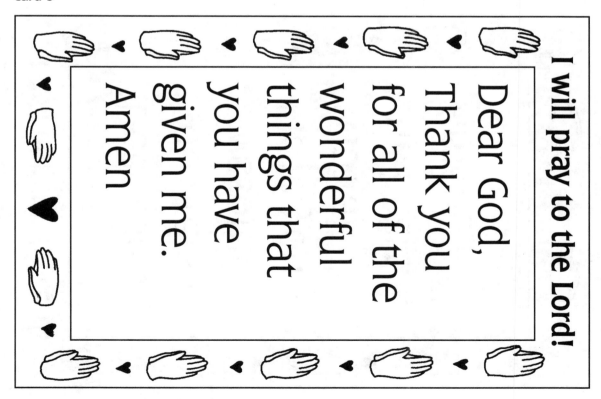

I will pray to the Lord!

Dear God,
Thank you
for all of the
wonderful
things that
you have
given me.
Amen

Prayer Power Cards Patterns

Card 4

Dear God,
You watched
over Daniel,
and I know
that you are
watching
over me.
Amen

I will pray to the Lord!

Card 5

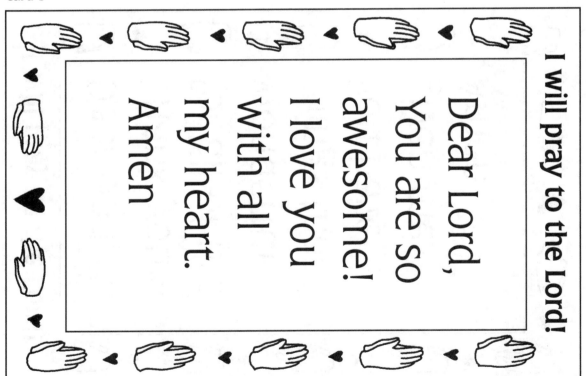

Dear Lord,
You are so
awesome!
I love you
with all
my heart.
Amen

I will pray to the Lord!

Prayer Power Cards Patterns

Card 6

I will pray to the Lord!

Dear Lord,
I will always
praise you
and worship
you.
I love you.
Amen.

Card 7

I will pray to the Lord!

Dear God,
I know you
are always
with me,
loving me,
and helping
me.
Thank you.
Amen.

The Big Fish Story

Jonah 1-4

Jonah learned that even though he did not always listen to God or do what God asked of him, God still loved him. God keeps loving us, even when we do not obey. This big fish and Jonah will help remind children that it does not matter where you go, God is always with you.

Materials Needed:

* ✳ 2 sheets of 12˝ x 18˝ blue or gray construction paper for each child.
* ✳ Glitter, crayons, or markers
* ✳ Stapler
* ✳ Glue
* ✳ Scissors
* ✳ Markers
* ✳ Newspaper – for stuffing
* ✳ White construction paper

Directions:

To make the fish:

1. Copy the big fish patterns found on pages 29 and 30. You will use these patterns as a stencil.
2. Place the front half of the fish together with the back half of the fish on a piece of construction paper and trace. (See illustration.) Each child should make two fish.
3. Cut out both fish.
4. Decorate the fish. You can use glitter, markers, paints, or crayons.
5. Place the two fish cut outs together, decorated sides out. Match the edges and staple along the edge of the fish where indicated on the pattern, leaving the bottom open for stuffing. (See illustration.)
6. Tear and crumple small pieces of newspaper and stuff into the fish.
7. Staple the opening at the bottom of the fish closed.

To make Jonah:

1. Copy the Jonah pattern found on page 31 onto white construction paper.
2. Color and cut out.
3. Roll the pattern until both sides meet at the dotted lines.
4. Staple or tape the pattern in place.
5. Jonah can now stand by himself!

2. Trace the fish pattern onto construction paper.

5. Staple sides together.

The Big Fish Story Pattern

Copy and cut out the front half of the fish. Use as a stencil.

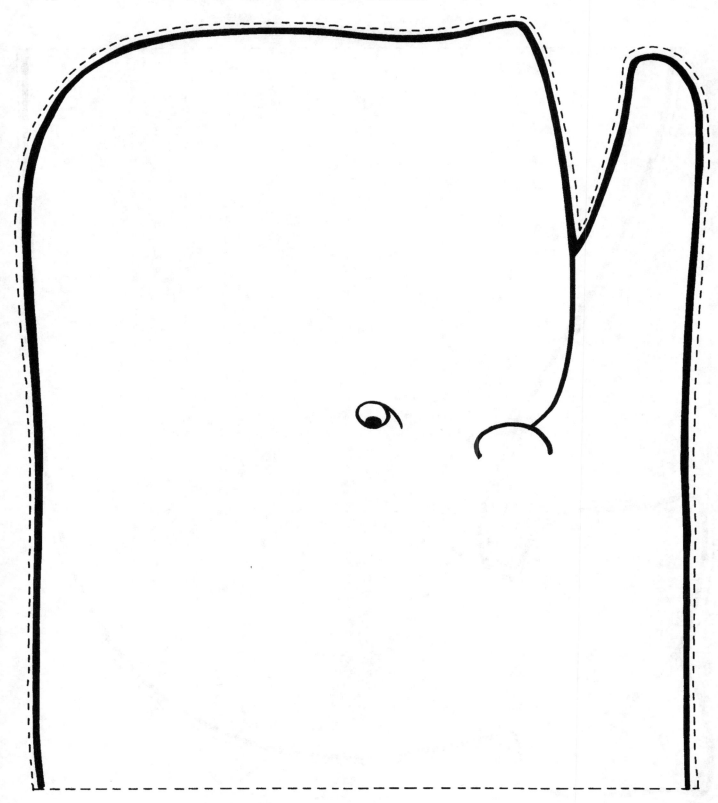

The Big Fish Story Pattern

Copy and cut out the back half of the fish. Use as a stencil.

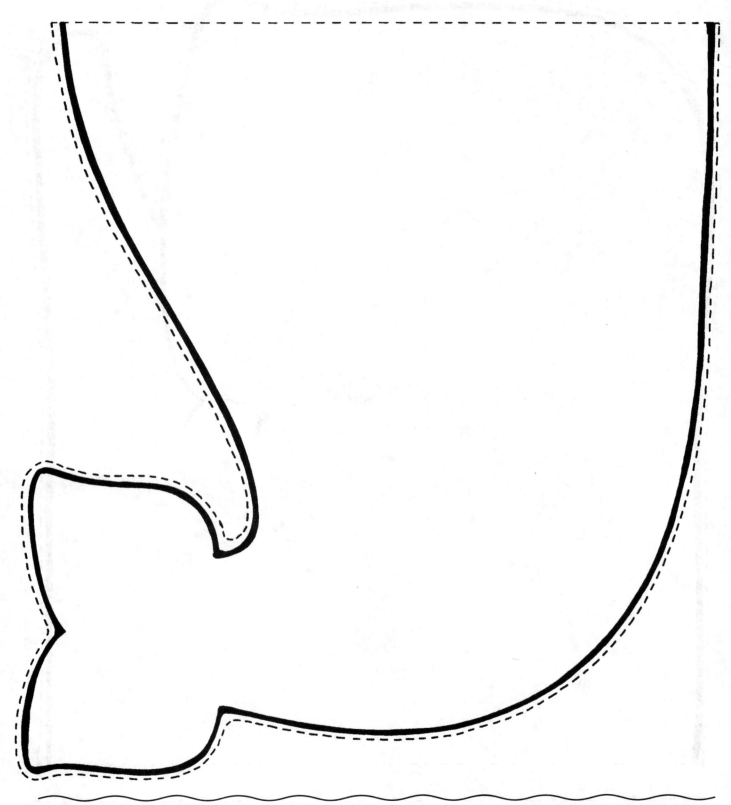

The Big Fish Story Pattern

Cut out Jonah along the solid line.
Roll and tape to secure.

The Great Escape

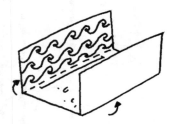

Exodus 13

God took care of Moses and led him to safety. The children will learn that God is here today to lead and guide them too. Children will get to help Moses and his people cross the Red Sea with this easy project.

Materials Needed:

* ✳ White construction paper or card stock
* ✳ Markers or crayons
* ✳ Scissors
* ✳ Gluesticks
* ✳ *Optional:* sand & glue

Directions:

1. Copy the Red Sea pattern found on page 33 for each child in your group.
2. Color the water blue and the ground brown. A fun option, which will create a more realistic Red Sea, is to brush glue on the ground area and sprinkle with sand. Let dry.
3. Fold along the dotted lines so the water is lifted up on either side of the ground.
4. Cut along the line indicated next to the water of the Red Sea.
5. Make two copies of each of the character patterns found on pages 34–35.
6. Color and cut out the characters.
7. With the back sides together, glue like characters to each other and fold along the dotted line.
8. Slide the character into the slit until character is standing on dry land.
9. Move/slide the character "across the Red Sea."

2. Color the water blue and the ground brown or sprinkle with sand.

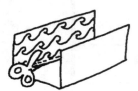

4. Cut a line to slide the characters.

3. Fold on dotted lines and lift sides.

9. Move/slide character "across the Red Sea."

7. Glue like characters to each other and fold on the dotted line.

The Great Escape Pattern

fold   fold

cut

fold   fold

The Great Escape Patterns

Make two copies of each character.

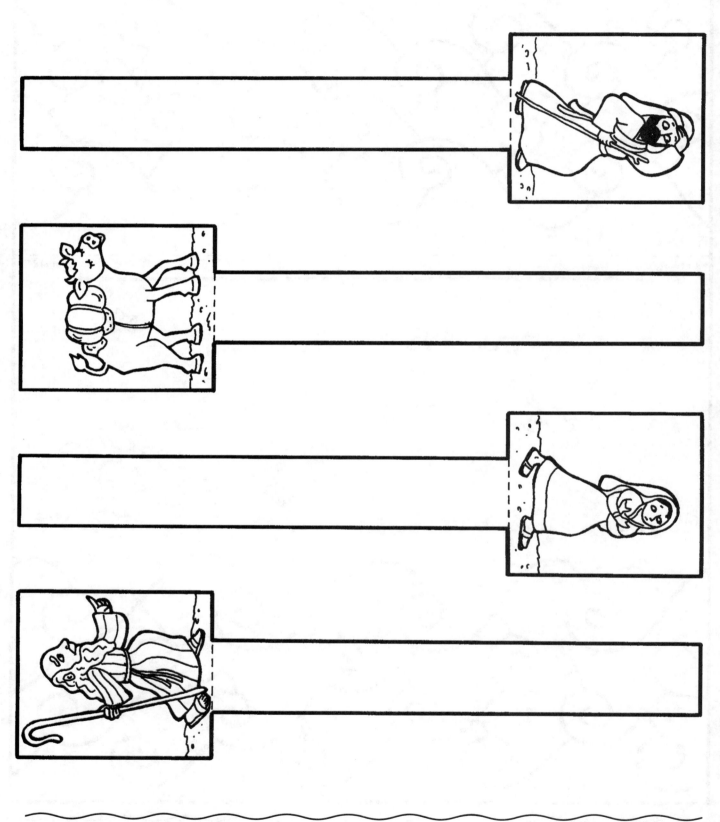

The Great Escape Patterns

Make two copies of each character.

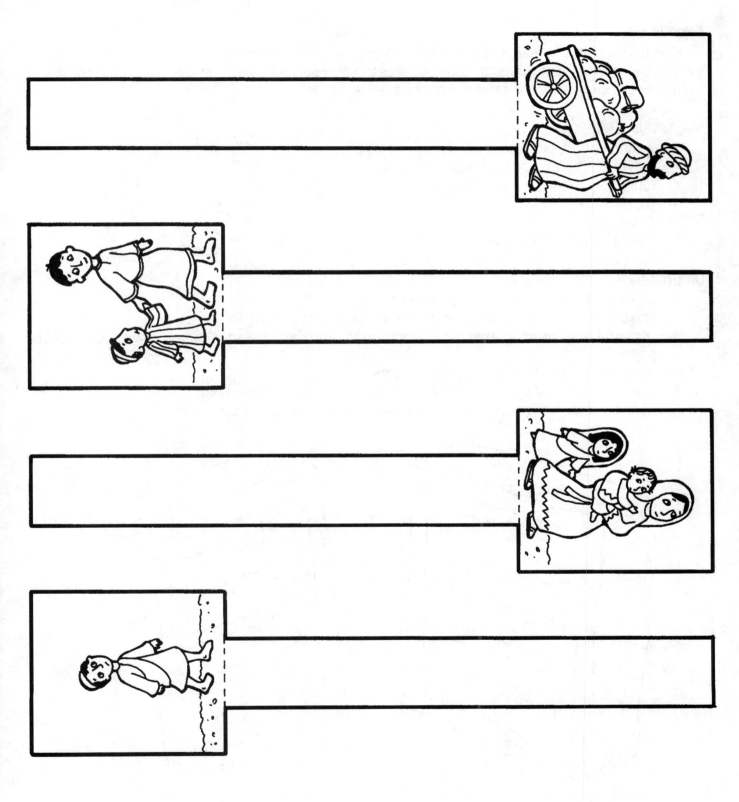

The Ten Commandments

Exodus 20

God gave Moses the first laws on tablets of stone. These laws are called the Ten Commandments. We use these commandments to guide our lives today. Help young children learn the Ten Commandments by creating the stone tablets from two cereal boxes.

Materials Needed:

* 2 cereal boxes per student
* Brown craft paper or brown grocery bags
* Glue
* Tape
* Scissors
* Brown construction paper

Directions:

1. Crumple the brown paper and flatten it so it looks "old."
2. Make the tablets by covering each cereal box with the crumpled paper.
3. Copy the Ten Commandments patterns found on pages 37 and 38 onto brown construction paper.
4. Cut out the Ten Commandments patterns.
5. Glue commandments one through five onto one covered cereal box.
6. Glue commandments six through ten onto the other covered cereal box.

1. YOU SHALL HAVE NO OTHER GODS BEFORE ME.

2. YOU SHALL NOT MAKE FOR YOURSELF AN IDOL.

3. YOU SHALL NOT MISUSE THE NAME OF THE LORD YOUR GOD.

4. REMEMBER THE SABBATH DAY BY KEEPING IT HOLY.

5. HONOR YOUR FATHER AND YOUR MOTHER.

6. YOU SHALL NOT MURDER.

7. YOU SHALL NOT COMMIT ADULTERY.

8. YOU SHALL NOT STEAL.

9. YOU SHALL NOT GIVE FALSE TESTIMONY.

10. YOU SHALL NOT COVET.

Exodus 20:3-17

Psalm Praise Banner

Psalm 150

Many of the Psalms tell us to praise the Lord! This celebration banner can be hung anywhere as a way to praise our wonderful and loving God.

Materials Needed:

* 12˝x18˝ colored construction paper
* String or yarn cut into 24 inch lengths
* Paper clip
* Scissors
* Glue
* Stapler
* *Optional:* assorted decorating mediums; paint, glitter, crayons, markers, sequins

Directions:

Banner verse: Let everything that has breath praise the Lord!
                            Praise the Lord! Psalm 150:6

1. Choose a colored 12˝x18˝ sheet of construction paper for your banner.
2. Create a fold 3/4˝ from the top and staple to make a 1/2˝ opening for yarn to slide through.
3. Copy the banner word patterns and decorations found on pages 39–41. Color and cut out.
4. Glue the words onto the banner in the order of the verse. Include the Bible reference.
5. Tie a paper clip to one end of the yarn.
6. Slide the yarn through the stapled opening using the paper clip as your weight/guide.
7. Tie the yarn ends together for a hanger.

Word patterns for Psalm 150:6.

Word patterns for Psalm 150:6.

Fun cut outs to decorate the banner.

Little Brown Stable

Luke 2

God's only son, Jesus, was born in a humble stable and laid in a manger because there was no room in the inn. Children love listening to and retelling the story of the birth of Jesus. Help your children learn the story and its meaning by creating the characters Mary, Joseph, Baby Jesus, a shepherd, sheep, donkey, cow, camel, and the Wise Men and by painting a simple shoe box and turning it into a stable.

Materials Needed:

* ✳ 1 shoe box per child
* ✳ Brown tempera paint and brush
* ✳ Sharp scissors or razor blade cutter (to be used by an adult)
* ✳ Card stock
* ✳ Markers
* ✳ Straw

Directions:

1. Cut out an opening on one side of the shoe box leaving no less than a 1˝ border on all three sides. (See illustration.)
2. Paint the outside of the shoe box brown and let dry.
3. Copy the characters on pages 43–45 onto card stock.
4. Color and cut out the characters.
5. Fold along the dotted lines so the characters will be able to stand.
6. Set characters in and around the stable and enjoy listening to the children retell the story of Jesus' birth.

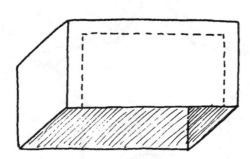

1. Cut out an opening on one side of shoe box.

5. Fold on the dotted lines so the characters will stand.

Copy and cut out cow, sheep, baby Jesus, and Mary.

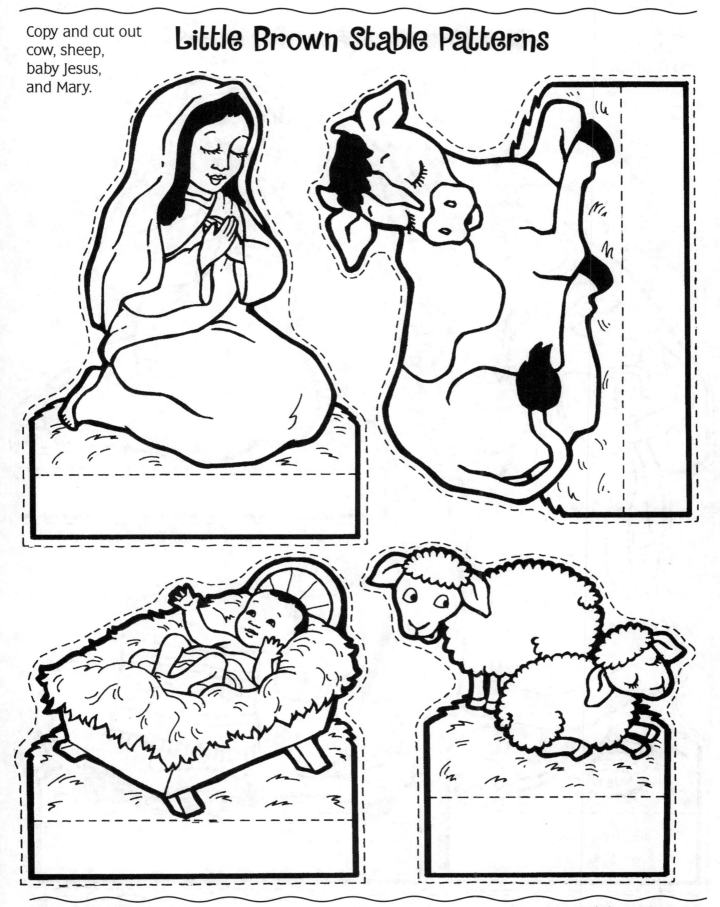

Copy and cut out
Joseph, donkey,
and shepherd.

Little Brown Stable Patterns

Little Brown Stable Patterns

Copy and cut out the Wise men and the camel.

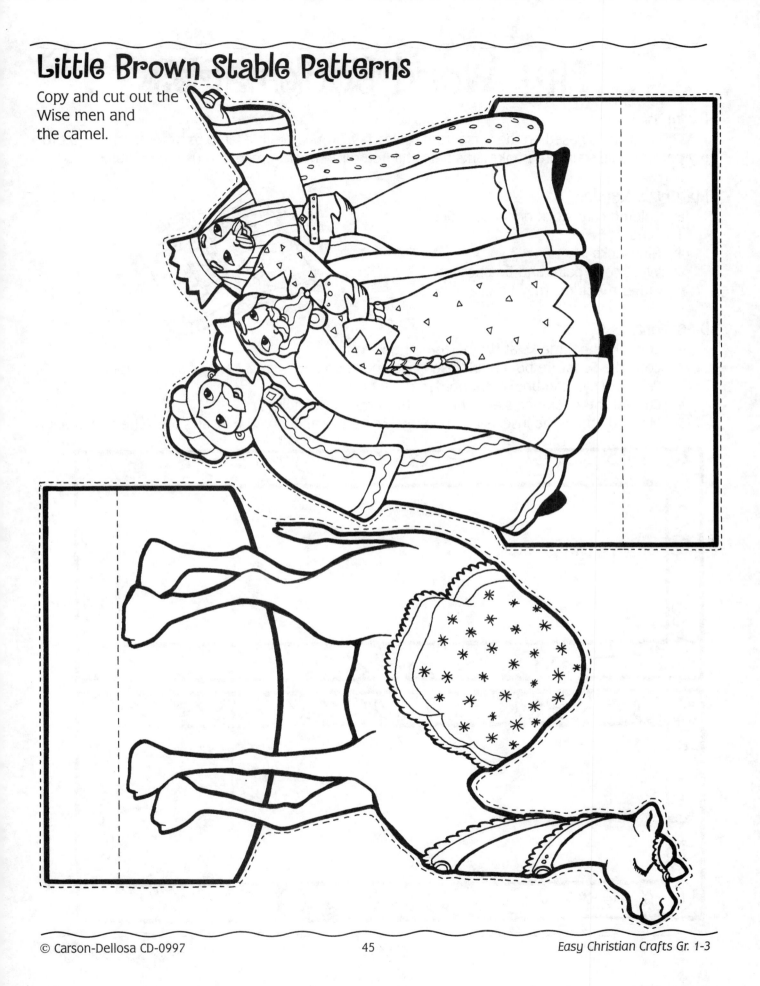

Thy Word Bookmarks

Psalm 119:105

This activity is based on the verse from Psalm 119: "Your word is a lamp to my feet and a light for my path." These scripture bookmarks help children remember to read and use their Bibles.

Materials Needed:

* Colored card stock or construction paper
* Scissors
* Gluesticks
* Watercolor paint and brushes (other mediums may be used)

Directions:

1. Copy the bookmarks at the bottom of this page.
2. Copy the Scripture bookmark insert patterns found on page 47 onto colored paper.
3. Paint or color the bookmark border and let dry.
4. Cut out the bookmarks and the inserts along the solid lines.
5. Mix and match the inserts and bookmarks. Center and glue the inserts onto the bookmarks.

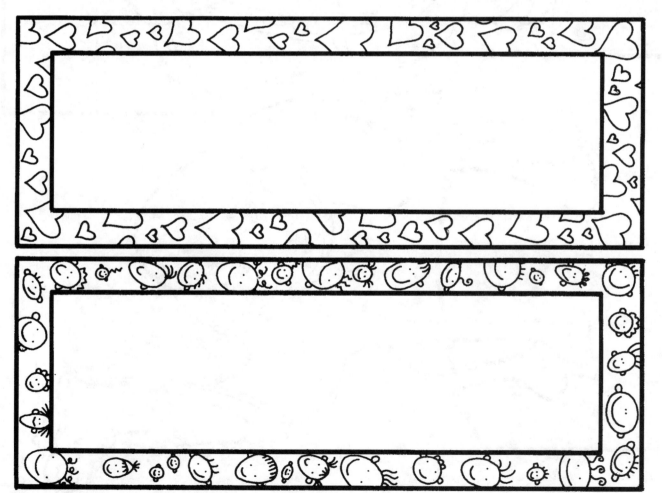

Thy Word Bookmark Patterns

Be wise and keep your heart on the right path.

Proverbs 23:19

Your word is a lamp to my feet.

Psalm 119:105

The joy of the Lord is your strength.

Nehemiah 8:10

A happy heart makes the face cheerful.

Proverbs 15:13

Fishers of Men

Matthew 4

Jesus tells us that if we love and follow him, he will help us tell others about him. That is what Jesus means by making us "Fishers of Men." Children will love making their own fishing pole and "catching" these special fish that show us various ways that we can tell others about God's love.

Materials Needed:

* Round or square magnets (bought at a hardware or craft store)
* String – cut into 36″ pieces
* Tape
* Eight paper clips per project
* Card stock or construction paper
* 30″ dowel, if possible, or let the children go outside and find a stick
* Scissors
* Crayons or markers
* Small plastic bag (sandwich size)

Directions:

1. Copy, color, and cut out the fish patterns found on pages 49 and 50.
2. Attach a paper clip to the top of each fish.
3. Wrap the string around one end of the "fishing pole" three times and tape in place.
4. Adjust the length of the string to the child fishing so the line will not get tangled.
5. Tape the other end of the string securely to the center of the magnet.
6. Place the fish on the floor and "catch" them!
7. Read how you can tell or show others about God's love.
8. Use a small sandwich bag to store the fish.

Fishers of Men Patterns

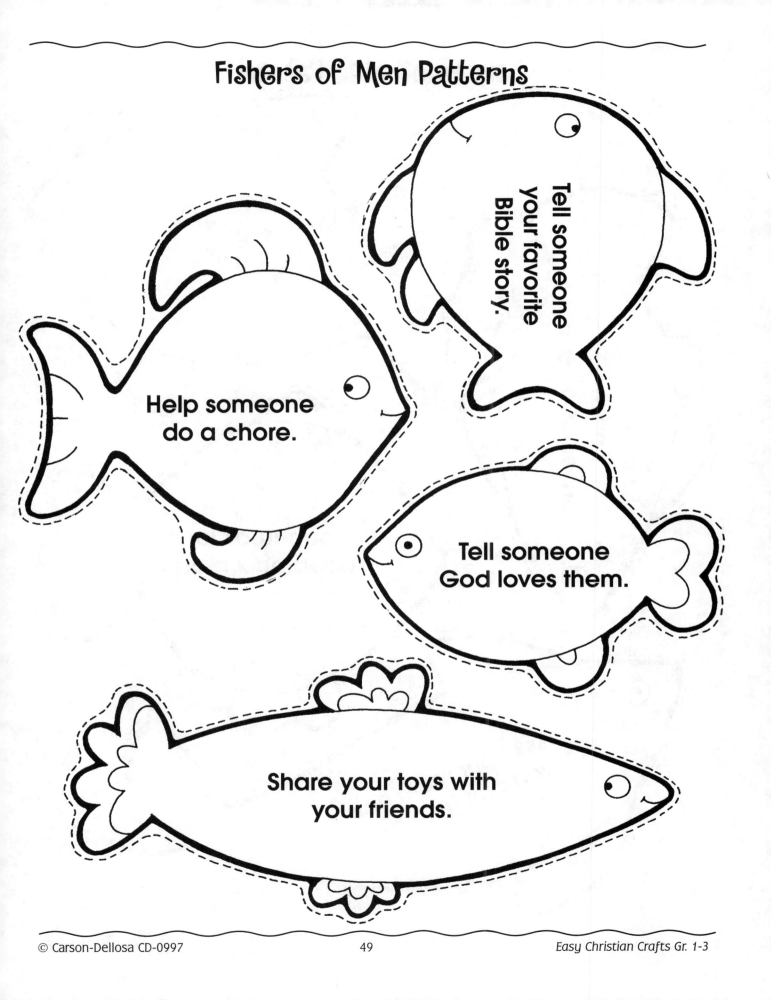

Tell someone your favorite Bible story.

Help someone do a chore.

Tell someone God loves them.

Share your toys with your friends.

Easy Christian Crafts Gr. 1-3

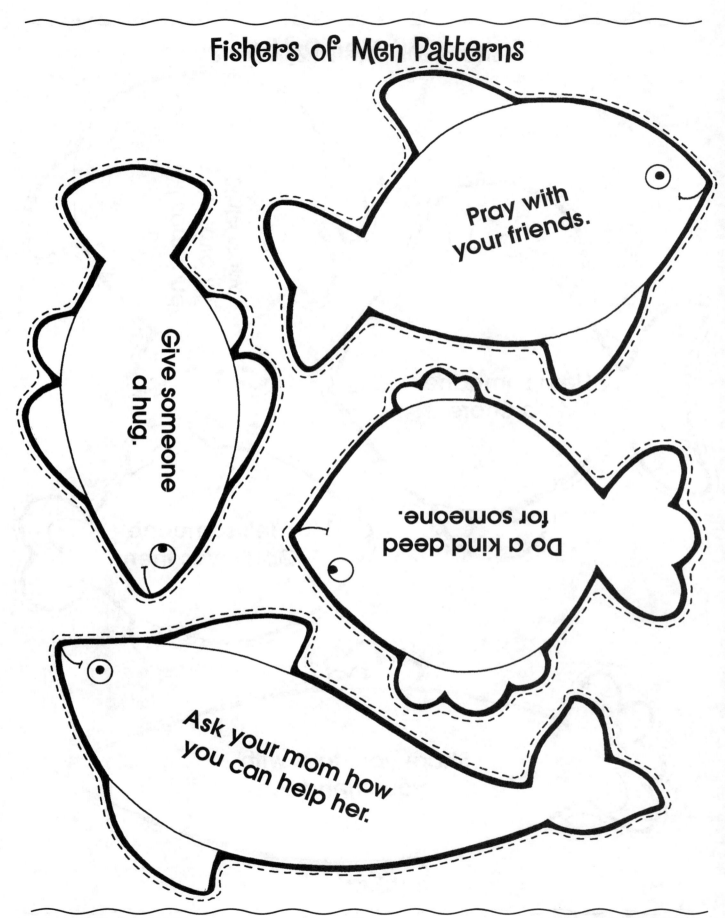

Pray with
your friends.

Give someone
a hug.

Do a kind deed
for someone.

Ask your mom how
you can help her.

Cinnamon Stick Cross

Matthew 27

Jesus died on the cross for each of us. These easy-to-make cinnamon stick crosses will remind children about how much God loves them.

Materials Needed:
* ✳ Two cinnamon sticks per cross
* ✳ 10˝ piece of brown embroidery floss or twine per cross
* ✳ Glue

Directions:
1. Position the cinnamon sticks to form a cross.
2. Glue the sticks together and let them dry.
3. Wrap the floss in a criss-cross pattern where the sticks intersect.
4. Tie a knot in the back of cross and cut the ends of the floss close to the knot.
5. If you want to hang the cross, before trimming floss, tie another loop in the floss for hanging.

Jesus Lives Wind Sock

Matthew 28

Jesus is alive! His resurrection promises us eternal life. Children can celebrate Easter every day with this windsock that will remind them that Jesus is indeed ALIVE!

Materials Needed:

* Two sheets of card stock or construction paper per wind sock
* Paper punch
* Six–16˝ pieces of yarn
* Markers or other medium for coloring
* Six–12˝ strips of crepe paper
* Stapler
* Tape

Directions:

1. Copy the wind sock patterns found on pages 53 and 54 onto card stock or construction paper.
2. Color and cut out the wind sock.
3. Line up the two pattern pieces where indicated and tape together on the back side.
4. To make the wind sock, roll the pattern to the indicated lines and staple or tape in place.
5. Punch holes where indicated at the top of the pattern using a paper punch.
6. Lace a piece of yarn through each hole, bringing the ends together evenly.
7. Hold all the ends of the yarn so your wind sock is suspended in air. Adjust the yarn so that the wind sock hangs evenly. Tie a knot holding them all together.
8. With a remaining piece of yarn, tie a loop for hanging.
9. Staple crepe paper streamers at the bottom of wind sock so they hang freely.

3. Line up the pattern pieces and tape.

4. Roll the pattern and staple or tape in place.

5. Punch holes.

6. Lace a piece of yarn through each hole and tie.

8. Tie a loop for hanging.

Jesus Lives Wind Sock Pattern

Fruit of the Spirit Tree

Galatians 5

Jesus said that if we live in him we will bear the fruit of his love. This simple fruit tree will help children learn the fruit of the Spirit and how Jesus wants to help us grow in our faith.

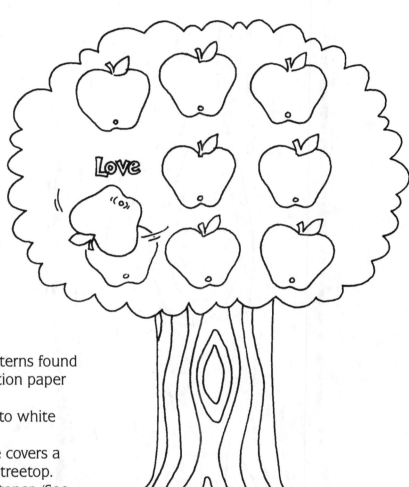

Materials Needed:

* ✳ Brass fasteners
* ✳ Crayons or markers
* ✳ Scissors
* ✳ Brown, green, and red construction paper

Directions:

1. Copy the tree trunk pattern found on page 56 onto brown construction paper and cut out.
2. Copy the treetop pattern found on page 57 onto green construction paper and cut out.
3. Make nine apples using the patterns found on page 56 out of red construction paper and cut them out.
   (The patterns can be copied onto white paper and then colored red.)
4. Position the apples so each one covers a "fruit of the Spirit" word on the treetop. Attach in place with a brass fastener. (See illustration.)
5. Attach the treetop to trunk with stapler or gluestick.
6. Rotate fruit to discover which fruit of the Spirit is hidden behind each apple.

4. Position apples so they cover each "fruit of the Spirit" word on the treetop and attach in place with a brass fastener.

Fruit of the Spirit Tree Patterns

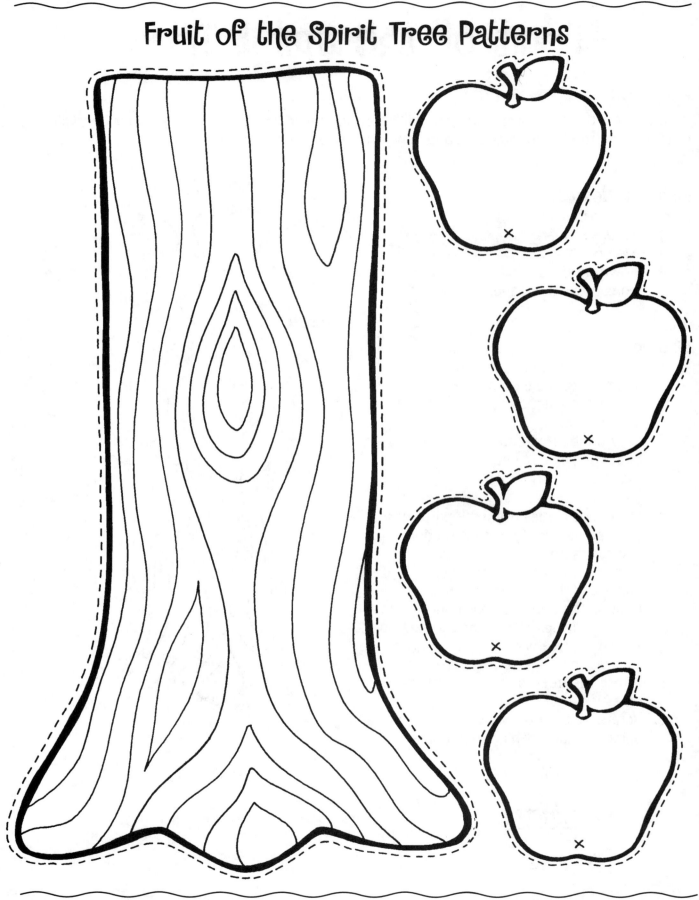

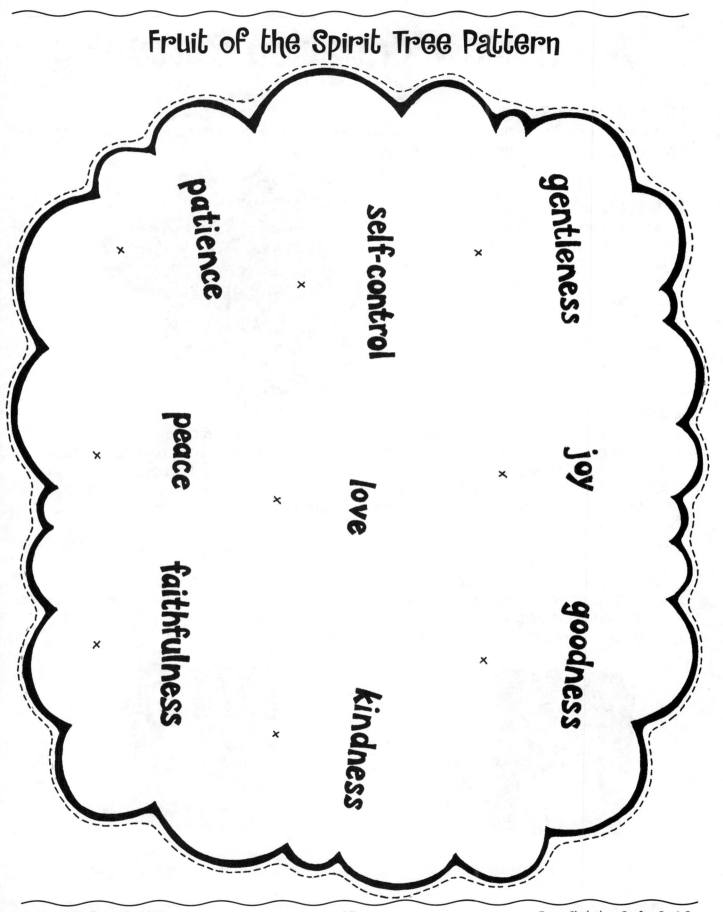

I Am a New Creation Butterfly

2 Corinthians 5:17

Just as a caterpillar changes into a beautiful butterfly, we also change and become a new creation when we make a commitment to Christ.

Materials Needed:

✳ Card stock to be used as templates
✳ Bright colored tissue paper
✳ 12″ x 18″ piece of black construction paper
✳ Chalk or white crayon
✳ Glue or gluestick
✳ Scissors

Directions:

1. Copy the butterfly pattern found on page 59 onto card stock and cut out.
2. Copy two butterfly wing insert patterns found on page 60 onto card stock and cut out.
3. Copy the Bible verse pattern found on page 60 onto card stock and cut out.
4. Glue the Bible verse onto the center bottom of the black construction paper as shown.
5. Using chalk or a white crayon, trace the main butterfly pattern onto the black construction paper.
6. Trace the wing insert onto the wing, then flip over to trace the same pattern on the other wing. Use the picture below as your guide.
7. Tear tissue paper into small pieces and crush into tiny balls
8. Glue tissue paper balls inside of wings pattern. (See the illustration of the finished project at the top of the page.)
9. Let dry and then cut around Bible verse and butterfly outline.

4. Glue Bible verse onto the center bottom of the black construction paper.

6. Trace the wing insert onto the wing, then flip over and trace the same pattern on the other wing.

I Am a New Creation Butterfly Pattern

Trace onto black paper.

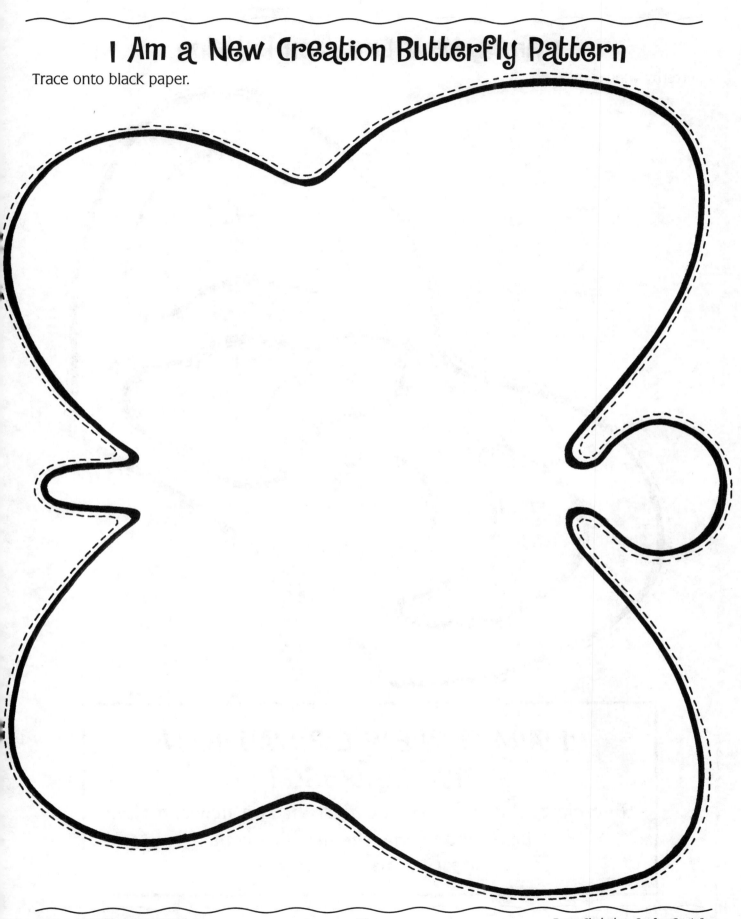

I Am a New Creation Pattern

Butterfly wing stencil

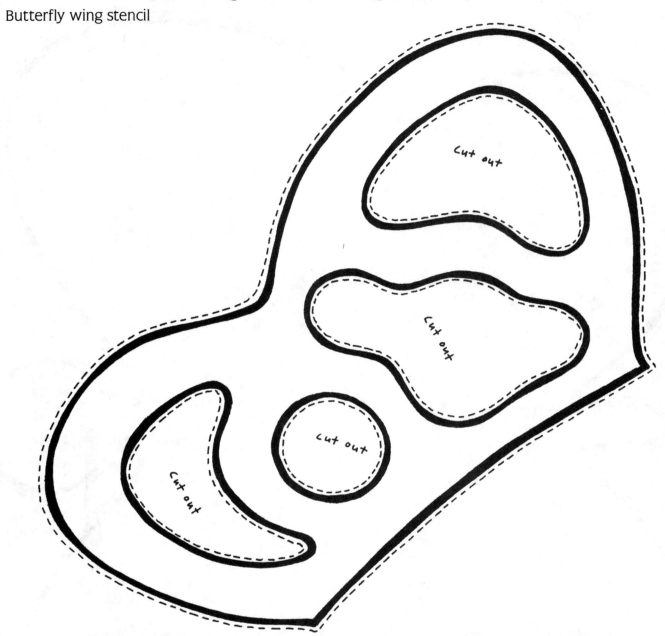

I AM A NEW CREATION
IN CHRIST!

*Therefore, if anyone is in Christ, he is a new creation;
the old has gone, the new has come!*
2 Corinthians 5:17

Armor of God Display

Ephesians 6

Paul gives us wonderful tools of truth to take with us each day to keep our faith strong. Children will make a two-sided armor display to help them learn and remember what the Armor of God is.

Materials Needed:

* ✶ Construction paper
* ✶ White copy paper
* ✶ Glue or gluesticks
* ✶ Scissors
* ✶ Paper punch
* ✶ Yarn cut into 6˝ lengths

Directions:

1. Make two copies of each pattern found on pages 62–64 on white paper. Color and cut out.
2. Make four copies of display band pattern found on page 63 on construction paper.
3. Glue double strips together where indicated on pattern. This will strengthen the display band.
4. Cut two 5˝ x 5˝ squares from six different colors of construction paper.
5. Mount each identical pair on the same color paper.
6. Cut around each shape, leaving a framed border of construction paper.
7. Line up one set of all the armor along one side of the strip and glue in place.
8. Turn entire strip over and glue the back of the matching armor shape to the back of its mate.
9. Punch a hole in the top center.
10. To hang your Armor of God display, string a piece of yarn through the top and tie.

feet planted in

PEACE

helmet of

SALVATION

Armor of God Display Patterns

sword
of the
SPIRIT

Display strip
copy 4

breastplate of
RIGHTEOUSNESS

Overlap and glue
at dotted line.